T0115157

SUPERFOOD COCKTAILS

DELICIOUS, REFRESHING & NUTRITIOUS RECIPES FOR EVERY SEASON

DEVON BROWN & ALANA MILLS

A POST HILL PRESS BOOK

Superfood Cocktails:
Delicious, Refreshing, and Nutritious Recipes for Every Season
© 2019 by Devon Brown & Alana Mills
All Rights Reserved

ISBN: 978-1-64293-090-0

Cover art by Cody Corcoran
Photography by Alana Mills
Interior design and production by Greg Johnson, Textbook Perfect

Post Hill Press
New York • Nashville
posthillpress.com

Published in the United States of America
Printed in China

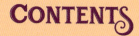

CONTENTS

INTRODUCTION

This crazy adventure began in the summer of 2017, when we became co-workers and fast friends. We instantly bonded over our mutual love of fashion, the winter Olympics, and, of course, cocktails. This love of fun and fruity drinks led to us continuously treating ourselves to various happy hours and brunches around Nashville. As most adults do in the new year, by winter 2018, we had both come to the realization that we wanted to get healthier. However, we didn't want to give up our time socializing with friends, which, like most twenty-somethings, is done with a cocktail in hand. So, we got to work researching how to turn our favorite hobby into something that fit in with our new, healthier lifestyle. And somehow, this book came to life!

Before we started this project, we were both aware of superfoods as the latest health craze sweeping the country. However, we had no idea just how many superfoods there were! We did a ton of research, and discovered not only all of the amazing things superfoods could do for us, but, most surprisingly, how many were already in our diet—from berries to citrus, and even a spice as simple as cinnamon. We also discovered a ton of unique superfoods, which are a little harder to find but worth the extra effort.

For those of you who have picked up this book by chance, welcome! We thought it might be a good idea to give you a little overview of what a superfood really is. A superfood, as defined by Merriam-Webster is, "a nutrient-rich food considered to be especially beneficial for health and well-being." While many superfoods also have individual health benefits (we'll get to that later), most foods in this powerhouse category have the common benefits of being high in antioxidants, good for lowering your blood pressure, good for heart health, and most even help to prevent cancer by fighting free radicals in the body. Each recipe in this book highlights a unique superfood and features some of the more interesting or surprising benefits we found along the way. This book is broken down by season to ensure you are getting the superfoods when they are in peak freshness or when their unique benefits will be most helpful. Clearly, we're not mixologists or health care professionals, just two friends sharing an old love of cocktails and a newfound passion for superfoods. We're excited to share with you how to get the most out of the foods you eat every day, while incorporating new favorites into your diet.

This project is filled with late night sessions, liquor store runs, Pinterest boards, and far too many experimental drinks to count. We hope you enjoy it and learn a thing or two along the way.

Cheers!

Devon & Alana

A Note on Ingredients

We based this collection around the seasons, highlighting ingredients when they are fresh for the healthiest possible drinks, but we know that it isn't always easy to get your hands on these ingredients.

We want this to be a fun and customizable experience and substitutions are always welcome!

Feel free to use frozen versions of any of the fruits when needed to enjoy these drinks year-round. If you don't have time for the fresh stuff, already pressed juice is perfect. We used a lot of nut milks in these recipes to cut down on the dairy, but you can always use your milk of choice. The same goes for sugars: feel free to substitute in raw sugar or coconut sugar where we use the real stuff.

Have fun with it!

Summer Cocktails

Smashed Blueberry & Mint Frozen Margarita

Kicking things off on a high note! Our queen of all superfoods, blueberries are packed with antioxidants and vitamins that make them not only a tasty treat, but also extremely good for you. This summer berry may help fight UTIs and reduce DNA damage, which can protect you against cancer. The perfect drink for when your body needs a flush!

Ingredients

(Serves 2–4)

2 cups blueberries, fresh or frozen

3 ounces lime juice

5 ounces tequila

1 Tbsp Mint Simple Syrup (see page 90)

2 cups ice

Fresh blueberries or mint leaves
   for garnish, optional

Sugar for rimming glass

Directions

1. Combine the blueberries and lime juice in a blender; process on high until smooth.

2. Add the tequila, Mint Simple Syrup, and 1 cup ice to the blender. Blend on high for 30 seconds. Continue adding ice and blending until it's the perfect, smooth consistency, for us, around 2 cups of ice.

3. Rim the glasses with sugar and fill them with the frozen blueberry margarita mixture. Top with blueberries and mint, if desired. Serve immediately.

Adapted from GimmeSomeOven.com

Superfood Piña Colada

Don't let this blue-green algae scare you! Spirulina is a great natural source of energy, but it is best known as being extremely effective in reducing anemia (an iron deficiency in the body). Helpful hint: We promise this drink tastes good—just maybe don't smell the spirulina before you add it in…

Ingredients

(Serves 4)

4 ounces white rum

1 (13.5-ounce) can coconut milk

1 tsp spirulina

2 cups ice

3½ cups pineapple chunks, frozen

6 ounces pineapple juice

Pineapple wedges for garnish, optional

Directions

1. Combine rum, coconut milk, spirulina, ice, frozen pineapple chunks, and pineapple juice in a blender. Purée on high until everything is combined, about 1 minute.

2. Pour into glasses and garnish with pineapple wedge.

Adapted from CaliGirlCooking.com

Strawberry Ginger Smash

It's no coincidence that strawberries are heart shaped. This well-known summer fruit helps to protect your heart and lower your blood pressure, while also increasing your "good" cholesterol. Also, while strawberries are full of natural sugars, they're actually very effective in helping both type 1 and type 2 diabetics manage their blood sugar.

Cocktail Ingredients

(Serves 1)

¼ cup smashed strawberries

2–3 shakes Angostura bitters

2 ounces bourbon

3 ounces ginger ale or ginger beer

Fresh mint and fresh strawberries
    for garnish, optional

Smashed Strawberry Ingredients

2 cups strawberries, hulled and chopped

1 Tbsp sugar

1 tsp fresh mint, chopped

½ tsp freshly grated ginger

2 ounces bourbon

Smashed Strawberry Directions

1. Place the strawberries into a medium-sized bowl and toss them with the sugar, chopped mint, and ginger. Let them sit at room temperature for 10 minutes.

2. Add the bourbon and mash the strawberries with a fork or muddler. Let sit for another 10 minutes before using. Can be stored in the refrigerator up to a week for future drinks.

Cocktail Directions

1. Add the strawberries to the bottom of a chilled glass and mash with the bitters. Add ice on top of the strawberries.

2. Pour the bourbon over the ice and top it off with ginger ale or ginger beer.

3. Garnish with fresh mint and fresh strawberries and serve.

Adapted from HowSweetEats.com

Raspberry Vodka Lemonade Slush

Raspberries, another top cancer-fighting food, is one of the best superfoods for women. This is due to high levels of fiber, which women specifically need to protect themselves against various cancers. Raspberries have also been shown to help improve overall memory and decrease the decline of cognitive abilities related to aging.

Ingredients

(Serves 10)

1 (6-ounce) can frozen orange juice, thawed

2 (6-ounce) cans frozen lemonade, thawed

2 (6-ounce) cans frozen limeade, thawed

1 cup sugar

3½ cups water

3 cups vodka

Chambord or Raspberry liqueur

Fresh raspberries for garnish

Directions

1. Combine orange juice, lemonade, limeade, sugar, water, and vodka.

2. Freeze 12 to 24 hours, stirring occasionally.

3. Fill serving glass with frozen vodka mixture.

4. Top with Chambord or raspberry liqueur and fresh raspberries.

Cherry Chia Mimosa

Cherries aren't just for Shirley Temples anymore! While also helping us sleep better, cherries are mostly known for their anti-inflammatory benefits, which include regulating heart rate and reducing soreness after exercise. Fun fact: tart cherry juice actually has a higher concentration of nutrients than whole cherries.

Ingredients

(Serves 4)

14 ounces 100% tart cherry juice, divided

4 ounces St. Germain

4 ounces seltzer water or club soda

2 Tbsp chia seeds

24 ounces champagne or sparkling white wine, chilled

Cherries, pitted for garnish, optional

Directions

1. Whisk 6 ounces of cherry juice, St. Germain, seltzer water or club soda, and chia seeds together.

2. Let the mixture stand until the chia seeds absorb the liquid, chill for about 20 minutes and whisk again before serving.

3. Add the cherry-chia mixture, champagne, and remaining 2 ounces of tart cherry juice to a glass. Stir gently to combine.

4. Remaining chia mixture can be refrigerated for up to 1 week.

Adapted from MammaChia.com

Watermelon Basil Mojito

Watermelon, a deceptively simple fruit, is full of vitamins, potassium, and magnesium, which makes it a proven stress reliever. Fun fact: because it is mostly made up of water, watermelon is a great way to keep hydrated on those hot summer days.

Ingredients

(Serves 1–2)

¼ cup fresh watermelon, chopped and seeded

2 basil leaves

1 ounce fresh lime juice

1 ounce Simple Syrup, store-bought or homemade (see page 90)

2 ounces white rum

Club soda to taste

Directions

1. Blend watermelon and lime juice on high until it is a smooth consistency.

2. In a glass, muddle the basil leaves with the Simple Syrup.

3. Strain muddled mixture into the blender and add the rum. Blend on high for at least 30 seconds.

4. Top with crushed ice and a splash of club soda.

Adapted from MammaChia.com

SUMMER COCKTAILS **13**

Chia Fresca

One of the most versatile superfoods because of its neutral flavor, chia seeds can be used in pretty much any recipe you can think of, which is great since it has so many amazing health benefits. Chia seeds are a great source of fiber, are high in protein, and are naturally non-GMO and gluten free—this makes them perfect for any dietary need. Fun fact: Chia seeds contain almost the same amount of omega-3 fatty acids as salmon, but no one wants to drink a salmon cocktail…

Ingredients

(Serves 1)

1 tsp chia seeds

1½ ounces tequila

1 ounce Aperol

1 ounce pineapple juice

½ ounce fresh lime juice

¼ ounce Simple Syrup, store-bought or homemade (see page 90)

Directions

1. Combine the tequila, Aperol, pineapple juice, lime juice, and Simple Syrup in a shaker and add ice. Shake vigorously for 20–30 seconds.

2. Strain into a short glass over a large ice cube.

3. Top with chia seeds and let sit for 5 minutes to hydrate chia.

Adapted from FoodRepublic.com

Peach Basil Bellini

Peaches are skin's best friend. Proven to help reduce wrinkles, improve overall skin texture, and fight against skin damage, peaches are a great way to help protect the skin against the harmful sun during the long summer months.

Ingredients

(Serves 4)

2 fresh peaches, peeled, pitted, and cubed

2–3 basil leaves

4 ounces Peach-Basil Simple Syrup (see page 91)

24 ounces Prosecco or champagne, chilled

Directions

1. In a medium glass bowl, muddle the peaches with the basil leaves.

2. Divide the peach-basil mixture into four glasses and add 1 ounce each of Peach-Basil Simple Syrup, or more to taste.

3. Top off each glass with prosecco or champagne.

Adapted from Heinen's Grocery Store

Blackberry Old Fashioned

Your dentist's superfood of choice, blackberries contain anti-bacterial and anti-inflammatory abilities that help fight against gum disease and could help prevent cavities. Blackberries are also one of the top cancer-fighting superfoods. This is because they contain high levels of anthocyanin, a pigment that is found in red, purple, and blue foods.

Ingredients

(Serves 1)

2 Tbsp Blackberry Simple Syrup (see page 91)

3 shakes orange bitters

2½ ounces bourbon

2 blackberries

Sparkling water

Directions

1. Combine the Blackberry Simple Syrup and orange bitters in an old fashioned or short glass.

2. Add the bourbon, ice cubes, black-berries, and a splash of sparkling water.

3. Stir to combine.

Adapted from TheSpruceEats.com

Frozen Tropical Refresher

This island fruit has some of the most diverse health benefits of any super-food highlighted in this book. Better even than orange juice, pineapple can help shorten colds by reducing congestion in the throat and nose. Pineapple is also helpful in preventing osteoporosis, especially in post-menopausal women. Fun fact: One serving of pineapple contains the recommended daily dose of vitamin C.

Ingredients

(Serves 4–6)

2 cups pineapple chunks, fresh or frozen

6 ounces pineapple juice

1 cup ice

2 cups coconut water, chilled

8 ounces vodka, chilled

2 ounces lime juice

1 lime, cut into wedges

Directions

1. Add the pineapple chunks and pine-apple juice to a blender. Blend on high until it is a smooth consistency. (If it's difficult to blend, go ahead and add lime juice or coconut water to blender.)

2. Add the ice, coconut water, vodka, and lime juice to blender. Blend until on high at least 30 seconds or until smooth.

3. Pour into tall glasses and squeeze lime wedge over each drink.

Adapted from FoodfromFlossie.com

Fall Cocktails

Blueberry & Sage Shrub

Not only is sage good for cleansing bad energy, it's also good for cleansing the body. Sage contains high levels of magnesium, a mineral directly linked to improving the quality, duration, and tranquility of sleep. Sage is also a great superfood for fighting or even delaying Alzheimer's disease.

Ingredients

(Serves 1)

2 cups blueberries, fresh or frozen

2 ounces apple cider vinegar

1 cup raw sugar

2 Tbsp sage, fresh

1½ ounce gin

Club soda

Directions

1. In a blender or food processor, combine the blueberries and vinegar. Purée until it's totally smooth.

2. Combine the blueberry purée with the sugar in a small saucepan over medium heat. Place the sage into a tea ball or wrap it up in some cheesecloth, then drop into the pot. Heat, stirring until the sugar is completely dissolved. Keep tasting the mixture and cook until the sage flavor reaches the strength that you want. This can take anywhere from 5–10 minutes.

3. Remove the blueberry-vinegar syrup from the heat and take out the sage. Transfer the shrub syrup to a container and refrigerate until ready to use.

4. Fill glass with ice. Add 2½ ounces of blueberry-vinegar syrup and gin to glass and top off with club soda.

Adapted from GlueandGlitter.com

Blood Orange-Blackberry Rum Punch

So good we had to highlight it twice! Blackberries have a later season, which makes them a great berry to star in your cocktails in both the summer and the early fall. One of the OG superfoods, blackberries tend to be looked over in favor of other fruits, like blueberries or raspberries. Blackberries, though, actually have a lot higher antioxidant content than many other foods. Paired with another superfood, blood orange, this drink is the perfect transition into the cozy fall months.

Ingredients

(Serves 6–8)

8 ounces blood orange juice, chilled

4 (12-ounce) cans blackberry soda, chilled

12 ounces white rum

3 ounces fresh lime juice

1 cup fresh blackberries

Mint for garnish, optional

Directions

1. In a large pitcher filled with ice, combine blood orange juice, blackberry soda, rum, and lime juice. Stir gently to combine.

2. Add several blackberries to each glass and pour the punch into the glasses. Garnish with more blackberries and mint, if desired.

3. Serve immediately.

Adapted from HeatherChristo.com

Fresh Ginger Moscow Mule

Along with the commonly known benefit of relieving nausea, ginger can also speed up the digestion process, helping relieve indigestion or related stomach disorders. A lesser known, but equally fascinating benefit of ginger—especially for our fellow ladies out there—is easing period pain. However, make sure to enjoy your ginger drink at the beginning of your cycle for maximum effect.

Ingredients

(Serves 1)

3 tsp grated ginger

1½ tsp sugar

4 basil leaves

2 ounces vodka

1½ ounces orange juice

1½ ounces fresh lime juice

4 ounces seltzer water

Lime wedge for garnish, optional

Directions

1. In a copper mug or cup, combine the ginger, sugar, and basil. Gently muddle for a few seconds until the basil releases its oils and becomes fragrant.

2. Add the vodka and stir well until the sugar completely dissolves.

3. Add the orange juice, lime juice, and a few ice cubes.

4. Top with seltzer water and give it a quick stir. Garnish with a lime wedge and enjoy!

Adapted from PickedPlum.com

St. Germain Cocktail

St. Germain is an elderflower or elderberry liquor. Elderberry is most famously used to treat cold and flu symptoms, specifically runny noses and congestion. This is because elderflower is an anti-catarrhal herb, which means it acts as a natural decongestant. Elderberries also act as a diuretic, which can improve kidney function and help treat symptoms of UTIs or bladder infections. This recipe is super simple, but the elderflower adds a powerful fruity-yet-floral twist!

Ingredients

(Serves 1)

2½ ounces St. Germain
   (or any elderflower liqueur)

3 ounces champagne or prosecco, chilled

1 ounce club soda

Directions

1. Pour the St. Germain and champagne or prosecco into a fluted glass over ice.

2. Top with club soda and stir well.

Turmeric Bloody Mary

Whether you think of tomatoes as a fruit or a vegetable, they are a super heart-healthy superfood. Tomatoes are a natural way to protect the inner layer of blood vessels, which is especially good for those who are prone to developing blood clots. Tomatoes are also really great for skin health and can help protect against sunburns. So, the next time you plan an outdoor adventure, make sure you drink your tomatoes so you don't turn into one.

Ingredients

(Serves 1)

5 ounces fresh tomato juice

2 ounces fresh carrot juice

2 Tbsp fresh lemon juice

½ tsp cracked black pepper

½ tsp turmeric

1 Tbsp basil, finely chopped

1½ tsp Worcestershire Sauce

3–4 drops olive oil

3 ounces vodka

Salt and turmeric for rimming the glass

Lemon wedges and celery for garnish, optional

Directions

1. Combine the tomato juice, carrot juice, lemon juice, black pepper, turmeric, basil, Worcestershire sauce, and olive oil in a pitcher. Stir in the vodka.

2. Combine the salt and turmeric on a shallow dish. Rub the lemon wedge on the rim of a serving glass, and dip in the salt mixture.

3. Add ice to the serving glass and pour the drink mixture over it. Garnish with another lemon wedge and a celery stalk, if desired.

Adapted from HelloGlow.com

Matcha Mojito

Matcha, while still fairly new in popularity in the US, has been used in Japanese tea services for centuries. Matcha is a powdered green tea, perfect to calm the mind and relax the body. Matcha has also been proven to help lower anxiety levels, so think of it as a soothing spa day in drink form.

Ingredients

(Serves 1)

2 tsp honey

1 Tbsp hot water

1 tsp matcha powder

1 lime, quartered

5 mint leaves

2 ounces white rum, chilled

3 ounces club soda, chilled

Directions

1. Pour the honey into a large glass (the one you plan on serving in), then add the hot water over top. Stir until you get a thinned honey water.

2. Add the matcha, and then mix with a spoon until the matcha is thoroughly incorporated and there are no lumps.

3. Squeeze the juice from each lime wedge into the honey mixture, then throw two of the quarters into the mixture. (Discard the other two quarters.)

4. Add the mint leaves to the matcha-honey mixture. Slightly muddle the leaves and juiced lime quarters with the back of a spoon.

5. Add the rum and a generous amount of ice cubes, then top off with club soda and give the mojito one last mix before serving.

Adapted from ThirstyforTea.com

Kale Cleansing Cocktail

We know that you're skeptical, but hear us out! Like many other superfoods, kale has lots of vitamins and antioxidants that help prevent cancer, specifically protecting against the formation of tumors. It is also really good for the eyes and can help drastically reduce the chance of cataracts. When you think of superfoods, most people automatically think of kale, but that doesn't mean you necessarily want to drink it—but just wait until you try this drink!

Ingredients

(Serves 1)

1 ounce vodka

1 ounce vermouth

¾ ounce Basil-Kale-Mint Simple Syrup (see page 92)

¾ ounce lemon juice

¼ tsp kale powder

4 dashes apple cider vinegar

Sparkling water, to taste

Lemon wedge, for garnish

Directions

1. In a chilled glass, combine the vodka, vermouth, Basil-Kale-Mint Simple Syrup, lemon juice, kale powder, and apple cider vinegar. Stir to combine kale thoroughly into drink.

2. Top with sparkling water and add a few ice cubes.

Adapted from FoodRepublic.com

FALL COCKTAILS   **37**

Açai Black Raspberry Cosmopolitan

One of the lesser known berries featured in our book, but one that has burst into the limelight in recent years, açai (Ah-sigh-EEE) berries are beneficial for pretty much every part of the body. Açai is good for increasing skin rejuvenation, preventing the growth of bad cancer cells, is energy boosting, and can assist in boosting brain function. Drink this powerhouse berry when you want an overall healthy kick.

Ingredients

(Serves 1)

2 ounces blueberry vodka

½ ounce Chambord or raspberry liqueur

½ ounce triple sec

2 ounces cranberry juice

½ tsp açai powder, dissolved in
    ½ ounce water

Fresh blueberries for garnish, optional

Directions

1. Add the blueberry vodka, Chambord, triple sec, cranberry juice, and dissolved açai powder into a cocktail shaker with ice.

2. Shake well for 20–30 seconds.

3. Strain into a chilled cocktail glass and garnish with a few fresh blueberries.

Adapted from TheSpruceEats.com

Super Switchel Cocktail

While many of the superfoods we chose to highlight in this book are fresh fruits or vegetables, we couldn't write a book about superfoods without including apple cider vinegar. While known for helping with weight loss and promoting healthy skin, apple cider vinegar also helps boost nutrient absorption and, coming from two people who struggle with sugar addiction, apple cider vinegar has been so helpful to reduce sugar cravings, since it helps keep blood sugar levels balanced. It is also worth mentioning that this is one of the least sweet and most "superfood-y" drinks in this collection.

Cocktail Ingredients

(Serves 1)

1½ ounces Apple Cider Mixture

3 ounces bourbon

Sparkling water, to taste

Apple slices for garnish, optional

Apple Cider Mixture Ingredients

6 ounces apple cider vinegar

8 ounces maple syrup

1 Tbsp fresh grated ginger

Apple Cider Mixture Directions

1. Place the apple cider vinegar, maple syrup, and ginger into a lidded jar.

2. Cover and shake well. Refrigerate for at least 2 hours..

Cocktail Directions

1. Pour 1½ ounces of refrigerated mixture over ice in a tall glass.

2. Stir in bourbon and top with sparkling water.

3. Stir to mix and garnish with an apple slice.

Adapted from BangorDailyNews.com

Maca Irish Coffee

We have to confess, this book is being written by two self-proclaimed coffee addicts. In fact, the majority of this book was written inside of a coffee shop! So, what better way to combine our two loves then by creating a spiked coffee cocktail. Featuring maca, a Peruvian root which you typically find in powdered form, this Irish coffee can help treat hot flashes and night sweats related to menopause. Most interestingly, maca can also help increase libido and fertility, and boost energy and endurance.

Ingredients

(Serves 1)

3 Tbsp coconut sugar

2 tsp maca powder

6 ounces strong brewed coffee

2 ounces Irish whisky

1 can full-fat coconut milk, refrigerated 24 hours, optional

½ tsp vanilla extract

1½ tsp pure maple syrup

Pinch of sea salt

Adapted from NavitasOrganics.com

Directions

1. In a small bowl, mix the coconut sugar with ¼ cup boiling water until it's dissolved. Add maca powder and a pinch of sea salt. Whisk until thoroughly combined.

2. Divide the coffee and whisky between two glasses and add 1 Tbsp of the coconut sugar mixture to each. Stir well.

3. Scoop out the thick top layer of chilled coconut milk, reserving the water part for another use. With an electric beater or stand mixer, beat the coconut cream on high speed for 30 seconds. Add the vanilla and maple syrup; beat until light and creamy, 1 to 2 minutes.

4. Top each glass with a few generous scoops of the whipped coconut cream.

Winter Cocktails

Green Juice Detox Margarita

Green Juice is made from combinating dark green leafy vegetables and a variety of other fruits and vegetables that are processed through a juicer. It's important to know that not all green juices are created equal. Benefits may vary depending on the green juice you choose and its ingredients. Not just a millennial fad, most standard green juices contain high amounts of vitamins C and E, which can help rid the skin of toxins and reduce acne. Green juice is also great for helping strengthen weak nails and hair and can even improve dark circles or bags under the eyes.

Ingredients

(Serves 3)

12 ounces green juice, store-bought or homemade

4 ounces fresh lime juice

6 ounces tequila

4 ounces triple sec

1–2 ounces Simple Syrup, store-bought or homemade (see page 90)

Lime for garnish, optional

Directions

1. Stir the green juice, lime juice, tequila, and triple sec together until blended. If you feel the margarita needs to be a little sweeter, add Simple Syrup to taste.

2. Serve over ice in sugar or salt rimmed glass, garnish with lime wedges or slices.

Adapted from GimmeSomeOven.com

Cranberry Mint Cape Cod

I bet every woman reading this already knows one health benefit of cranberry juice, but did you know that it has so many benefits for other parts of the body as well? Cranberry juice is proven to help boost metabolism, lower risk of heart disease, ease digestive issues, and lower blood pressure. Cranberries also contain anti-bacterial properties that can prevent bacteria from sticking to the teeth thus preventing gum disease.

Ingredients

(Serves 1)

1 ounce Mint Simple Syrup (see page 90)

4 ounces cranberry juice

2 ounces vodka

2 ounces fresh lime juice

2 ounces ginger ale

Sugared cranberries for garnish, optional

Directions

1. Combine the Mint Simple Syrup, cranberry juice, vodka, and lime juice in a shaker. Stir well.

2. Pour into tall glass filled with ice. Top with ginger ale and garnish with mint leaves and sugared cranberries.

Boozy Cacao Peppermint Hot Chocolate

Here it is ladies and gentlemen, proof that chocolate can be good for you! Cacao, which is made from the same plant as cocoa—just processed differently—contains more calcium than cow's milk and is the highest plant-based source of iron in the world. This antioxidant rich substance is proven to be a mood booster and a natural anti-depressant. Drink this when you need a mental boost heading into the crazy holiday season.

Ingredients

(Serves 8–10)

16 ounces vanilla almond milk, sweetened

3 ounces 100% cacao chocolate

3 Tbsp milk chocolate

2 ounces peppermint schnapps

2 ounces vanilla vodka

Pinch of salt

Peppermint candy for garnish, optional

Stove Top Directions

1. Combine sweetened vanilla almond milk, cacao, and milk chocolate in a saucepan, heat on medium heat until the chocolate is fully incorporated into the milk, about 6 minutes.

2. Let the chocolate cool partly, about 5 minutes.

3. Combine chocolate mixture with peppermint schnapps and vanilla vodka.

4. Serve in a mug topped with crushed peppermint candy, if desired.

Slow Cooker Directions

1. Combine sweetened vanilla almond milk, cacao, and milk chocolate in a slow cooker, and simmer on low heat for 2 hours. Stir occasionally.

2. Once all of the cacao and milk chocolate is incorporated into the milk, add in peppermint schnapps and vanilla vodka. Store in slow cooker to maintain heat, but be sure not to burn off the booze!

Orange Turmeric Margarita

Known by beauty fans for its bright orange color and skin-brightening properties, turmeric is one of the only spices featured in this book. Turmeric, which is pretty much anti-everything (anti-bacterial, anti-fungal, anti-inflammatory, anti-aging), supports whole body health and immunity. It can also improve brain function and has been shown to help fight against depression.

Ingredients

(Serves 1)

2 ounces tequila

2 ounces triple sec

3 ounces fresh orange juice

2 ounces Turmeric Simple Syrup (see page 92)

Orange slices for garnish, optional

Salt and turmeric, for rimming the glass

Directions

1. Fill a cocktail shaker with ice and add the tequila, triple sec, orange juice, and Turmeric Simple Syrup. Shake vigorously for 20–30 seconds.

2. Rim the glass with a mixture of salt and turmeric.

3. Serve with an orange slice, if desired.

Adapted from VintageKitty.com

Sweet & Spicy White Russian

I would bet that almost everyone reading this book has cinnamon in their pantry right now. Cinnamon is one of the most commonly known and used superfoods highlighted in this book, but there are a lot of health benefits associated with it that you might not know about. Cinnamon, when used correctly, is great for helping to regulate blood sugars in diabetics. This is due to cinnamon reducing the bodies resistance to insulin. It also helps boost immunity and fight against respiratory infections. Drink this when you feel a winter cold coming on.

Ingredients

(Serves 1)

1 ounce vanilla vodka

½ ounce Kahlua

½ ounce heavy whipping cream

1½ tsp cinnamon

Cinnamon stick or ground cinnamon, for garnish

Directions

1. Combine the vanilla vodka, Kahlua, cinnamon, and heavy whipping cream in an ice-filled shaker.

2. Shake vigorously for 20–30 seconds.

3. Pour over ice in a short glass and garnish with cinnamon stick or a sprinkle of ground cinnamon.

Adapted from WaitingonMartha.com

Pear Brandy Milk Punch

While pears are fairly mild in flavor, they pack a powerful fiber punch. In fact, pears are great for helping to treat many common chronic conditions that are associated with low fiber diets, like diverticulosis. And, in an ironic twist, pear juice has also been proven to help reduce hangover symptoms. So, make sure to keep any leftover juice on hand in case you enjoyed this cocktail a *little* too much.

Cocktail Ingredients

(Serves 2–4)

12 ounces vanilla almond milk, sweetened

4 ounces brandy

4 ounces pear juice

Pinch of nutmeg

Brandied Pear Ingredients

8 ounces brandy

¼ cup brown sugar

1 ripe pear, seeded and diced

Brandied Pear Directions

1. Add brandy and brown sugar into a medium saucepan. Cook over medium heat until brown sugar is dissolved.

2. Add in diced pear and continue cooking over medium heat for 5 minutes, turning the pears a few times as they cook. Be sure not to turn the heat too high as they might flambee!

Cocktail Directions

1. Combine sweetened vanilla almond milk, brandy, pear juice, and nutmeg in a cocktail shaker. Shake for 20–30 seconds.

2. Layer brandied pears into the bottom of a glass and top with the brandy-pear juice mixture.

3. Top with a sprinkle of nutmeg.

Pink Grapefruit Paloma

One of the more traditional drinks in this collection, a typical paloma is made up of tequila and grapefruit juice. So, while you may have had one or two palomas in your day, you probably weren't aware of the benefits of this delightful, citrusy drink. Grapefruit contains high amounts of citric acid, which can help lower the risk of developing kidney stones. Grapefruit is also a natural pain reliever, so this is the perfect brunch cocktail after a night out with friends.

Ingredients

(Serves 2)

3 ounces tequila

5½ ounces pink grapefruit juice, freshly squeezed

Kosher salt

2 ounces grapefruit-flavored sparkling water

1 ounce Simple Syrup, store-bought or homemade (see page 90)

½ ounce lime juice

Lime wedges for garnish

Directions

1. Combine tequila and grapefruit juice in a cocktail shaker filled with ice.

2. Shake well for 20–30 seconds.

3. Pour the tequila-grapefruit mixture over ice cubes into serving glass, squeeze a lime wedge over it, and top with grapefruit sparkling water.

Pumpkin Irish Cream

Not just for Thanksgiving anymore, pumpkin is a great seasonal superfood to add to any winter cocktail. One of the best benefits of pumpkin is that it may help reduce the risk of cancer, specifically breast cancer, due to high levels of beta-carotene. Pumpkin is also really great for your eyes! Rich in vitamin A, which helps prevent chronic eye diseases, this holiday staple can also help to strengthen teeth and bones.

Ingredients

(Serves 3)

5 ounces sweetened condensed milk

12 ounces Irish whisky

8 ounces sweetened vanilla almond milk

3 Tbsp pumpkin purèe

1 tsp espresso powder

1 tsp pumpkin pie spice

1 tsp vanilla extract

Directions

1. Combine all ingredients in a blender, blend on high until smooth.
2. Serve in a mug, either cold or warmed up.

Adapted from ArisMenu.com

Blood Orange Mulled Wine

The optimal window for blood oranges is very short (we're talking three weeks) in the early winter months, but the health benefits are so great— and this cocktail is *so* dang delicious—we had to include it anyway. Though similar to a regular orange, a blood orange is special because it combines the common benefits from both orange and purple foods due to the interesting, rich color. One of the coolest things about a blood orange is that it helps the body protect and heal itself from outside toxins, which could be anything from prolonged exposure to cigarette smoke to city pollution. So, the blood orange is the superhero of the superfoods...a *super* superfood if you will.

Ingredients

(Serves 6)

½ bottle of red wine, preferably Lambrusco or a fairly sweet red

12 ounces apple cider

5 ounces blood orange juice

Mulling spices (ours contained cinnamon, orange peel, allspice, cloves, ginger), homemade or store-bought

1 orange, sliced

1 blood orange, sliced

1 lime, sliced

Directions

1. Combine wine, apple cider, orange slices, blood orange slices, lime slices, and mulling spices in a medium saucepan. Heat the mixture just barely to a simmer over medium-high heat.

2. Reduce heat to medium-low, let wine simmer for 15–20 minutes. (You can leave it on low heat for up to 3 hours.)

3. Strain out the spices and fruit and serve. For a big batch version, double the recipe and combine all ingredients in a slow cooker and heat on low for 2 hours.

Pomegranate Mimosa

While once difficult to find, now pomegranate seeds can be found at most local supermarkets, which is great because they have so many unique health benefits that were previously much harder to take advantage of. Pomegranate seeds and pomegranate juice both increase testosterone levels in men and women, which makes it a great natural aphrodisiac and fertility aid. Pomegranates can also protect against breast cancer and prostate cancer, which makes it a beneficial superfood for both men and women. Fun fact: pomegranate juice has about three times more antioxidants than red wine.

Ingredients

(Serves 4)

16 ounces pure pomegranate juice, chilled

8 ounces fresh orange juice, chilled

4 ounces triple sec

1 bottle prosecco or any sparkling wine, chilled

Pomegranate seeds for garnish, optional

Directions

1. Gently mix the pomegranate juice, orange juice, and triple sec in a large pitcher.

2. Fill a champagne flute three-fourths full with prosecco.

3. Fill the rest of the glass with the pomegranate juice mixture and stir gently.

4. Top with pomegranate seeds, if desired.

Spring Cocktails

Fresh Banana Margarita

We know what you're thinking...bananas? But, actually bananas were one of the OG superfoods. Full of fiber and potassium, bananas slow digestion, keep you fuller for longer periods of time, and can help regulate your heart rate. Another benefit of bananas, which most people already know, is that because they contain such high amounts of potassium, they are great to help treat muscle cramps.

Ingredients

(Serves 3)

2 medium-sized bananas, sliced

½ cup pineapple chunks, frozen

2 ounces fresh lime juice

4 ounces tequila

4 ounces triple sec

1 cup ice, plus more if needed

Sliced banana for garnish, optional

Directions

1. Add bananas, pineapple, lime juice, tequila, triple sec, and ice to a blender. Blend on high until it is a frosty consistency.

2. Pour the banana mixture into salt or sugar rimmed serving glasses.

3. Garnish with banana slices.

Adapted from womensrunning.com

Fizzy Matcha Ginger Kombucha

Not gonna lie, before taste testing this recipe, neither of us had actually tried kombucha before (we know, we know, we were late to the party). However, after trying it, we were hooked! Kombucha, which is a fermented tea beverage, is best known to help regulate digestion since it's full of built-in probiotics. Kombucha also contains high amounts of iron and vitamin B, which makes it an energy booster and natural mood enhancer. Fun fact: Kombucha can naturally contain trace amounts of alcohol due to the fermentation process. Use this recipe to boost the alcohol content!

Ingredients

(Serves 1)

3 ounces vodka

2 tsp honey

1 Tbsp water

½ tsp matcha powder

1 lime, cut into wedges

6 ounces ginger kombucha

Fresh mint for garnish, optional

Directions

1. Mix the honey with one Tbsp of water and stir to combine until you have a thinned honey water.

2. Combine the vodka, honey water, and matcha powder in a cocktail shaker. Shake 20–30 seconds until the matcha dissolves completely. Add ice and shake for another 15–20 seconds.

3. Fill one chilled glass with ice and pour the matcha-vodka mixture over the ice.

4. Squeeze the juice from a lime wedge into each glass. Fill the rest of the glass with ginger kombucha and garnish with a few mint leaves. Serve immediately.

Adapted from HowSweetTreats.com

The Celery Cure

The perfect alternative to a Bloody Mary, this earthy cocktail is a great addition to your next post-night-out brunch. If the fact that eating celery uses up more calories than is *in* the vegetable wasn't enough to entice you, celery, ironically, helps protect against liver disease and can boost overall kidney health. Another sign that this is the perfect hangover cure: celery is also proven to help reduce bloating and limit water retention. So drink up, but be warned—this is not one for the celery haters out there!

Ingredients

(Serves 1)

3 ounces dry gin

1½ ounce fresh lime juice

1 ounce Simple Syrup, store-bought or homemade (see page 90)

1 ounce fresh celery juice

Celery stalk for garnish, optional

Directions

1. Combine gin, lime juice, Simple Syrup, and celery juice in a cocktail shaker. Fill to the brim with ice, and chill by gently inverting the cocktail shaker about 10 times.

2. Strain into a chilled glass, and garnish with celery stalk.

Adapted from PopSugar.com

Avocado Daiquiri

Coming from huge fans of the avocado-margarita craze, we knew we had to include avocado in this book. It's the perfect addition because avocados have so many health benefits, we couldn't even list them all. First and foremost, avocado is a heart-healthy fat. So much so, in fact, that the fat in avocados could actually help you dramatically increase the amount of nutrients you're absorbing from other plant-based foods. Avocado is also a great way to keep hair shiny and healthy due to the vitamin E content. Fun fact: Avocados also contain more potassium than bananas.

Ingredients

(Serves 2)

2 ounces white rum

2 ounces dark rum

½ ounce fresh lemon juice

½ ounce fresh lime juice

2 ounces Simple Syrup, store-bought or homemade (see page 90)

½ medium-sized ripe avocado, pitted and peeled

½ ounce half-and-half

1½ cups ice

Directions

1. Combine the white and dark rums, lemon juice, lime juice, Simple Syrup, avocado, half-and-half, and ice in a blender. Blend on high until it's smooth, about 30 seconds.

2. Divide mixture between two cocktail glasses and serve immediately.

Adapted from Epicurious.com

Red Hot Chile Pepper & Pineapple Cocktail

One half of this author duo loves this cocktail…the other half, not so much (that half is not a fan of spicy foods). We will start by saying this cocktail does have some kick to it, but the hot peppers featured in this drink are actually the best part. While the benefits of chiles do seem counterintuitive, many of the vitamins and minerals in these peppers are actually very good for the heart and stomach. In fact, chiles can prevent the formation of stomach ulcers and can prevent artery shrinkage, which can lead to heart attacks and strokes. This is due to chiles containing high levels of capsaicin. Another interesting benefit of chiles is that they are natural pain relievers. So, eat some chiles to help relieve the pain of eating chiles?

Ingredients

(Serves 1)

1 red chile pepper, seeded and sliced into rings

1 ounce vodka

2 ounces mango rum

6 ounces pineapple juice

Pineapple wedges and pepper rings for garnish, optional

Directions

1. Drop the chile pepper rings into a cocktail shaker.

2. Pour in the vodka and mango rum and add ice. Shake vigorously for 1 minute.

3. Add the pineapple juice and give a few more shakes.

4. Strain into a glass filled with ice and garnish with pineapple wedge and peppers.

Adapted from ChiliPepperMadness.com

Goji Berry Rickey

Skip the fillers and drink some goji berries instead. One of the more under-rated superfood berries, goji berries are great for their anti-aging properties. They have been shown to prevent damage to collagen in the skin, which is the main cause of wrinkles. Goji berries are also known to help boost immunity to help fight against the flu. Fun fact: although less popular in the US, goji berries have been used in traditional Chinese medicine for over two thousand years! Be careful though, it works so well that sometimes it can interfere with other medicines, so be sure to check online before adding too much to your diet.

Ingredients

(Serves 1)

1½ ounce vodka

1½ tsp goji berry powder

½ ounce agave syrup

¾ ounce fresh lime juice

Sparkling water, to taste

Lime wheels for garnish, optional

Directions

1. Whisk goji berry powder with vodka and let sit for 15 minutes.

2. Combine the goji berry-vodka mixture, agave syrup, and lime juice into a cocktail shaker.

3. Shake well for 20–30 seconds, then pour into a glass.

4. Top with sparkling water, and garnish with a lime slice, if desired.

Adapted from Mandatory.com

Cucumber Mint Collins

Light and refreshing, cucumbers aren't just for a spa day. One of the most surprising benefits we found for cucumbers while researching this book is that they can actually help cure bad breath. This is because certain chemicals in cucumbers kill the bacteria that causes this embarrassing faux pas. Cucumbers are also 96 percent water, so they are a perfect way to stay hydrated while helping to replenish the body of nutrients lost during the day.

Ingredients

(Serves 1)

9 mint leaves

3 (¼-inch) cucumber slices

½ ounce Simple Syrup, store-bought or homemade (see page 90)

1½ ounce gin

½ ounce fresh lemon juice

¾ ounce lime juice

2 ounces seltzer water, chilled

Directions

1. Muddle the mint leaves with the cucumber in the bottom of a serving glass.

2. Add the Simple Syrup, gin, lemon juice, and lime juice. Stir to combine. Fill the glass with ice, top with seltzer, and stir gently to mix.

3. Garnish with more mint leaves and a thin cucumber slice, if desired.

Adapted from SeriousEats.com

Carrot, Orange & Rhubarb Rum Cocktail

Most people, especially in the south, associate rhubarb with strawberry rhubarb pie—but this spring leafy vegetable can also shine in other settings (mainly cocktails). Rhubarb, commonly described as "red celery," is great for helping you lose weight by making your body burn fat faster. It is also a great source of calcium for vegans and is rich in iron and vitamin K, which helps the production of new red blood cells. Helpful hint: **Do not** eat the leaves, they are poisonous—only eat rhubarb stalks! If you are concerned, most grocery stores carry frozen rhubarb, so you can avoid the stress altogether.

Ingredients

(Serves 2–4)

¾ cup raw carrots, peeled and sliced

1 orange, peeled and seeded

½ cup raw rhubarb, peeled and chopped or frozen (only the stalk—*we repeat, do not eat the leaves)*

1 Tbsp maple syrup

4 ounces water

4 ounces orange juice

2 ounces almond milk, unsweetened

1 cup ice

4 ounces white rum

Directions

1. Combine the carrots, orange, rhubarb, maple syrup, orange juice, almond milk, water, rum, and ice in a blender.

2. Blend on high until smooth, about 30 seconds.

Adapted from GreenBlender.com

Iced Moringa Latte

Once again embracing our love of coffee-based cocktails, this moringa latte is packed with so many vitamins and minerals that are beneficial to the body and the mind. Moringa has blood-clotting properties, which means it can shorten the amount of time it takes for everyday scratches and cuts to stop bleeding. It also might help to fight against infections, such as salmonella and E.coli thanks to anti-bacterial and anti-fungal properties.

Ingredients

(Serves 1)

2 ounces 2% or skim milk

1 ounce vanilla vodka

1 ounce Kahlua

1 tsp moringa powder

½ tsp vanilla extract

Directions

1. Add milk, vodka, Kahlua, moringa powder, and vanilla extract to a shaker.

2. Shake 20–30 seconds or until moringa powder is complete dissolved.

3. Strain into serving glass, over ice.

Honey Lavender Bees Knees

Honey, the superfood that needs no introduction. Well regarded as one of nature's best sweeteners, honey is a great substitute for processed white sugar; however, keep in mind that, while healthier, honey is still high in calories and will raise your glycemic index the same as white sugar. Honey is also great to use as a natural cough suppressant, and in some cases, can be even more effective than cough medicine. Fun fact: If you purchase honey made in the region you live, it can help reduce allergy symptoms. This is due to the natural pollen found in honey.

Ingredients

(Serves 1)

1 tsp honey

1 ounce fresh lemon juice

2 ounces gin

4 ounces lavender soda

Directions

1. Add the gin and honey to a shaker and stir to dissolve the honey.

2. Add in lemon juice.

3. Fill shaker with ice and shake for 20–30 seconds.

4. Strain into a coupe glass and top with lavender soda.

Adapted from GastronomBlog.com

Simple Syrups

Simple Syrup

Ingredients

1 cup water

1 cup sugar

Directions

1. Bring water to a boil. Add the sugar and whisk into the boiling water. Continue the whisking until the sugar is completely dissolved.

2. Remove from heat and allow to cool. Refrigerate until ready to use.

3. Bonus: this can be made with raw sugar for an even healthier drink.

Mint Simple Syrup

Ingredients

1 bunch of fresh mint

1 cup water

1 cup sugar

Directions

1. Rinse mint leaves until clean.

2. Bring water to a boil. Add the sugar and whisk into the boiling water. Continue whisking until sugar is dissolved.

3. Add the mint and boil for 1 minute.

4. Remove from heat and let the mint steep for about 30 minutes as the syrup cools. Using a slotted spoon, remove the mint from the syrup.

5. Pour the cooled syrup through a fine mesh strainer into storage container. Refrigerate until ready to use.

Peach-Basil Simple Syrup

Ingredients

1 cup sugar

1 cup water

1–2 basil leaves

2 peaches, pitted and sliced

Directions

1. Bring water to a boil. Add the sugar and whisk into the boiling water. Continue whisking until sugar is dissolved.

2. Stir in basil leaves and peaches.

3. Remove from heat. Cool at room temperature for about an hour, letting the basil and peaches steep.

4. Strain and refrigerate in a sealed container until ready to use.

Blackberry Simple Syrup

Ingredients

1 cup blackberries, ripe

¾ cup sugar

1¼ cup water

Directions

1. Combine the blackberries, sugar, and water in a small saucepan. Over medium-high heat, simmer for 10 minutes. Reduce the heat if it starts to boil.

2. Remove from heat and mash the blackberries.

3. Cool at least 10 minutes, and then strain through a fine-mesh strainer into sealed container. Squeeze as much syrup through the strainer as possible. Refrigerate until ready to use.

Basil-Kale-Mint Simple Syrup

Ingredients

1 bunch basil

1 bunch kale

1 bunch mint

1 cup prepared simple syrup

Vodka

Vanilla extract

Directions

1. Bring water to a boil. Mix in the basil, mint, and kale leaves. Boil for 30–60 seconds. Immediately transfer the herbs to a bowl of ice water.

2. Once the herbs are cool, remove from ice bath and dry on a paper towel.

3. In a blender, combine the herbs with the prepared simple syrup.

4. Add a few dashes of vodka and vanilla extract.

5. Strain well and refrigerate until ready to use.

Turmeric Simple Syrup

Ingredients

1 cup sugar

1 cup water

1 Tbsp turmeric

Directions

1. In a small sauce pan, combine the sugar, water, and turmeric.

2. Place over medium heat and bring to a boil.

3. Cook until sugar dissolves.

4. Strain the syrup through a fine mesh strainer and refrigerate until ready to use.

A Final Note

Firstly, we want to say thanks so much to our readers! We hope that you enjoyed our quirky and fun descriptions and the recipes we ended up with as much as we loved testing them.

This book started as a crazy idea for a healthier happy hour and ended up as the product of many many hours of passion and dedication you have just finished. We couldn't be happier with the final product!

We do want to emphasize that we aren't trained medical professionals and, while all of the foods listed in this book are known to offer these benefits, the results are not immediate and will vary depending on the person. But the hope for this book is to enlighten you all to the everyday benefits of fruits, veggies, and spices that you probably already have in your diet and introduce you to some new and more obscure foods that are really beneficial.

We hope you discovered a new favorite cocktail or even a healthier twist on an old classic.

Cheers to many more healthy-*ish* cocktails!

ACKNOWLEDGMENTS

There are so many people who have played a part in getting this book completed. First off, we want to thank Anthony Ziccardi and Michael L. Wilson for believing in our vision for this project! We are very thankful to work for a publisher who encourages creativity, independence, and the power of a good cocktail. We greatly appreciate Billie Brownell for helping research and gather recipes, many of which we were ecstatic to try.

A huge thank you to Case Selects Wine & Spirits in Franklin, Tennessee, for being our go-to liquor store. We started many a Friday night at this store, and they were probably a little concerned until we told them we were writing a book!

Thank you to Madeline Sturgeon, Sarah Heneghan, Fiacha Heneghan, and Rachel Hoge for their support (and snacks) and their willingness to taste test all of our crazy recipes. Our monthly cocktail parties were the most fun we've ever had working, and helped shape the creative direction of this book. An extra special thank you to Sarah for loaning us many of the styling pieces seen throughout the book.

Thank you to Susan Brown for her styling assistance and willingness to let us take over her living room on multiple occasions, and Beck Brown, for his support and inventive cocktail ideas. Thank you to Sean & Laura Mills for their encouragement, and for the use of the camera (without which this project would have been a little trickier). Thanks also to Katie Mills for her enthusiasm and unending support and for sharing the news of our new project with everyone as soon as we shared it with her. It wouldn't be the same without you! We cannot wait for all of you to see the final product you have been so instrumental in building.

And lastly, we want to say thank you to each other. Alana, thanks so much for being the best partner in this project. I feel like this experience has truly strengthened our friendship. Your brilliant creative eye, and absolutely beautiful photos really made this book what it is. I am so thankful for you! Devon, this has been such a journey from start to finish and I wouldn't have wanted anyone else to be my partner in crime! Thanks for letting me take over your house every weekend and move everything around for the perfect shot. Thanks for being the bartender to my photographer and remaking the drinks multiple times until we got what we wanted. I can't believe this book is finally done and I can't wait for the next part of this adventure!

ABOUT THE AUTHORS

Devon Brown and Alana Mills are two co-workers turned best friends who, while not professional bartenders, are professional cocktail enthusiasts. In a quest to get healthy, but not miss out on happy hour, they decided to write a book infusing healthy ingredients into fun, flavorful cocktails.

When not testing new recipes, Devon and Alana spend their time in Nashville, TN, shopping, photographing, and daydreaming about their upcoming joint lifestyle blog.